CREATE
Colorful ALUMINUM
Jewelry

UPCYCLE CANS INTO VIBRANT NECKLACES, RINGS, EARRINGS, PINS, AND BRACELETS

Helen Harle

KB
KALMBACH BOOKS

Kalmbach Books
21027 Crossroads Circle
Waukesha, Wisconsin 53186
www.Kalmbach.com/Books

Published in 2010
14 13 12 11 10   1 2 3 4 5

Manufactured in the United States of America

ISBN: 978-0-87116-404-9

Publisher's Cataloging-in-Publication Data

Harle, Helen.
    Create colorful aluminum jewelry : upcycle cans into vibrant necklaces, rings, earrings, pins, and bracelets / Helen Harle.

    p. : ill. ; cm.

    ISBN: 978-0-87116-404-9

    1. Jewelry making--Handbooks, manuals, etc. 2. Art metal-work--Handbooks, manuals, etc. 3. Charms (Ornaments)--Handbooks, manuals, etc. I. Title.

TT212 .H28 2010
745.5942

CONTENTS

PROJECTS

INTRODUCTION

I have always been interested in crafts and enjoy trying new techniques. The thrill of creation is wonderful—but I don't like to spend a lot of money on tools and materials.

With cost control in mind, I started to look for inspiration in unusual places. When I thought about the bright colors and patterns on aluminum cans, I realized that they could be a wonderful resource for making jewelry and accessories, and I was thrilled to discover that they cut easily with scissors and ordinary paper punches designed for card making. You can manipulate the shapes with your fingers and pliers, and add beads and jewelry findings to make necklaces, earrings, bracelets, and much more.

This is a new craft you can start today! Aluminum cans are everywhere, and you may already have some of the tools you need. Work at the kitchen table, and make quick, colorful projects. Start with some of the simpler projects to get the hang of the techniques involved. If you have made jewelry before, you may know how to string beads or make a loop on wire. People who have done scrapbooking or card making are used to punching shapes and gluing pieces together.

Tell your family and friends to try new drinks "because I really need a can in that color!" Today we are asked to reduce waste, and I love the fact that I can make attractive jewelry out of discarded items—it's good for the planet and the soul. I hope you enjoy making these projects as much as I have.

MATERIALS AND TOOLS

CHOOSING CANS

The main material used in these projects is colored aluminum from drink cans. Drink cans are made from either steel or aluminum; use only aluminum cans. If in doubt, test with a magnet. If the magnet sticks, the can is steel and can't be used. Most cans are brightly colored and have printing or patterns that can be incorporated into the jewelry you make. If you want to use plain colors, try to find cans with large unprinted areas.

BEADS

I prefer to use **glass beads** in my jewelry, as they come in many shapes, sizes, and colors, including flower and leaf shapes. Larger beads can be strung on beading thread or combined with chain to make necklaces embellished with blossoms.

Seed beads are very small beads. Size 15 (also written as 15º) beads are the smallest, and size 6º are the largest (they make good flower centers).

When buying beads, look for ones that are smooth and well finished. Some cheap beads have rough edges that can damage the thread. Don't worry if beads are not all identical, as this adds to the handmade quality of your work.

FINDINGS

Findings are the components that jewelry makers use to assemble their jewelry. They can be made from many different metals including gold, sterling silver, copper, and brass. Less-expensive findings are made from steel and plated with silver or gold, and these work fine for these projects. Choose the color that goes best with your color scheme.

Head pins are short lengths of wire with a flattened end, like a large pin without a point. String beads and punched shapes onto them to make dangles. 1½–2-in. (3.8–5 cm) head pins are long enough for most projects. **Eye pins** are like head pins, except they have a plain loop at one end instead of a flat pad.

Jump rings are small rings that can be opened to join pieces together. They range from 2–20 mm in diameter, and they come in many colors. You can use 5–7 mm jump rings for the projects in this book.

Ear wires are the hook part of earrings. There are also post varieties that have a separate back.

Clasps are the fasteners for necklaces and bracelets. Lobster claw and spring ring clasps are attached to one end of a necklace and fasten into a jump ring at the other end. Toggle clasps have a loop and a bar; attach one half of the clasp to each end of a necklace or bracelet.

Chain is available in lots of different shapes and weights, and is sold by the foot or ready-made into necklaces and bracelets. I usually use simple curb or cable chain.

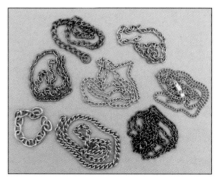

Craft wire is available in many different colors and gauges. In the US, thickness is measured by gauge; in Europe, by the diameter in millimeters. I use 24–28 gauge (.5–.315 mm) wire in these projects. Be careful if using pliers with colored wire, as the color can rub off.

Rivets, also called snaps, are small metal tubes that join pieces together without glue. I use flat-head rivets designed for card making. They are about ⅛ in. (3 mm) in diameter. They come in several colors and are very useful for joining multi-layered flowers. You can also use eyelets, if desired.

Ring findings either have loops to attach head pins or flat pads for gluing. Both types are used in this book.

Bracelet blanks are ready-made bracelets with flat pads where you can glue on decorative items. Choose the color and style that complements your design.

Pendant pads are flat plates with a loop attached for threading onto chain. Glue your decorative items onto them to make a pendant. Small ones can be used for earrings. Some have a hole in the center so you can rivet pieces together through the middle.

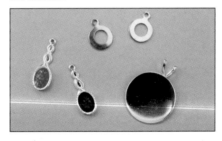

Sieve findings are usually made of two parts: a disk with small holes to sew through, and a solid backing piece that affixes to the disk after you have finished decorating it. There are different types of sieves, including brooches, rings, bracelets, and pendants.

TOOLS

All the tools you need are available from craft shops, hardware stores, and on the Internet. I bought a great paper-crafting set that included several of the items listed below, or you can buy them individually.

Ordinary, small paper-cutting **scissors** work fine for general cutting. There are many **paper punches** available for paper crafts, but simple shapes work best. In this book I have only used 10 different shapes, but once you have made a few projects, try some new punches and let your imagination flow. If the punch has a flap underneath to catch the punched shape, remove it, since you will usually be using the punch upside down and the flap gets in the way. Aluminum will not dull the punches much; I have used mine for two years, and they still make sharp, crisp images.

Use a **cork mat** when you need a soft surface, or for making holes with the needle punch, and use a **self-healing mat** for hammering shapes flat.

A small, lightweight **hammer** is handy for flattening and punching. Use a **needle punch**, a fine-pointed tool with a handle, for making small holes. You could use a large ordinary needle instead if you are careful when hitting it.

A metal **hole punch** and **eyelet tool** with interchangeable ends makes small holes in punched shapes for rivets or jewelry findings. Unscrew the ends to quickly change the hole size, or to set rivets or eyelets.

Choose pairs of **chainnose and round-nose pliers** designed for jewelry making. Use them for opening and closing jump rings, shaping flowers, and making loops. Use **wire cutters** to trim head pins and other lengths of wire.

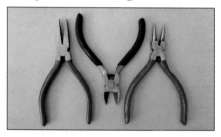

Smooth sharp edges with a fine **file**.

Choose gel-formula **superglue** for making double-sided shapes and **two-part epoxy glue** for attaching findings.

TECHNIQUES

PREPARING CANS

Wash cans thoroughly and let dry. Holding the can horizontally on a firm surface, use a short-blade knife to cut around the top of the can, just below the shaping. Push the blade carefully in and down. Always be VERY CAREFUL when cutting cans, as they have sharp edges. You may need to finish the cut with scissors. Turn the can around and cut off the bottom in the same way.

You now have a cylinder. Look carefully at the design on the can and decide the best place to cut vertically so you can get at the area you want to use. (Next to the printing/bar code panel works well.) Using scissors, cut the can vertically and open it flat.

Hold one cut end firmly, face-down onto your work surface, near the edge of the bench. Pull the free end downwards over the edge to curl the metal in the opposite direction. Turn the can around and repeat. The can should now be fairly flat.

PUNCHING SHAPES

Working on a firm surface, hold the punch upside-down and slide it onto the prepared can over the area you want to cut out. If you want a plain color, try to avoid any printing (although including the printing in a design can be fun). You can use the color variations on the can to enhance your shapes. For example, cutting leaf shapes from an area where green shades from light to dark gives the leaves depth and texture.

PUNCHING HOLES

To join pieces together, you will need to punch holes in the metal shapes. Make small holes for head pins with a needle punch. Place the shape on a cork mat, position the needle tool, and hit it firmly with a hammer. Turn the shape over onto a firm surface and tap with the hammer to flatten any sharp edges.

Make larger holes for jump rings or rivets with a hole punch. Place the shape on a self-healing mat, position the hole punch, and tap firmly with a hammer. You may need to hit it several times to punch right through. I find it helps to keep the punch clear by poking the scrap bits out of the center with a large needle every two or three cuts.

If you make the holes too close to the edge, the metal will break, as shown in the leaf on the left of the photo. The leaf in the middle is OK, but the one on the right has a perfect hole, evenly centered and about 1 mm from the edge.

FILING AND SHAPING

If there are rough edges on the punched shapes, smooth them using a fine file. Hold the shape against your finger and gently file over the edge, away from you. Then file along the edge until it is smooth.

Once you have filed the shapes, you can curve and fold them easily. If you pull a shape between your thumbnail and first finger, it will curve downwards. This is useful for shaping flower petals.

You can also curve petals over a pencil or pen, or use roundnose pliers to make a tight curl.

When folding shapes, be careful to get the fold in the right place the first time, as a badly placed fold will leave a mark in the metal that you can't remove.

RIVETING

Choose the pieces you want to join and punch out a hole large enough to fit a rivet or eyelet. Place the rivet head down on a self-healing mat, and layer the shapes on it, face down. Fit a riveting end to your eyelet tool, center it in the back of the rivet, and tap firmly with a hammer. This will curl over the edge of the rivet and make the join. Once the rivet is set, you may want to gently tap the back to get rid of any rough edges.

GLUING

To make double-sided shapes, use gel formula superglue, which is fast-acting and easier to control than liquid super-glue. Be careful not to get it on your fingers—I rub petroleum jelly on my fingers to keep stray glue from sticking.

Before gluing, hammer the shape flat. Hold the cut shape carefully by the edges, silver side up. Apply a thin, even layer of glue to the surface, taking it close to the edges. Lightly place a matching shape on top of the first shape. Position the top shape carefully before pressing the pieces together, as you can't move it once the glue sets.

To attach finished pieces to findings, such as hair clips or brooch backs, use two-part epoxy glue. Mix according to the manufacturer's instructions and apply sparingly with a toothpick. Let dry.

WIRED LEAVES

To make wired leaves, cut out a pair of leaf shapes and hammer them flat. Cut a piece of thin wire, place on a firm surface, and hammer about ⅝ in. (1.6 cm) flat at one end. Place one leaf shape on your cork mat, hold the flat-tened wire on the center of the leaf, and tap gently to make a dent in the leaf.

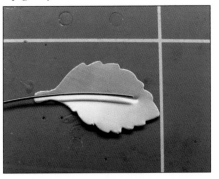

Squeeze a little superglue in the dent and fix the wire in place.

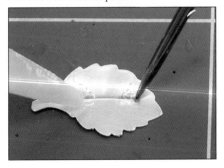

Spread more glue over the rest of the leaf and on the wire, and carefully place another leaf shape on top. Press down firmly to secure.

MAKING A PLAIN LOOP

1 Trim the wire or head pin ⅜ in. (1 cm) above the top bead. Make a right-angle bend close to the bead.

2 Grab the wire's tip with round-nose pliers. The tip of the wire should be flush with the pliers. Roll the wire to form a half circle. Release the wire.

3 Reposition the pliers in the loop and continue rolling.

4 The finished loop should form a centered circle above the bead.

MAKING A WRAPPED LOOP

1 Make sure you have at least 1¼ in. (3.2 cm) of wire above the bead. With the tip of your chainnose pliers, grasp the wire directly above the bead. Bend the wire (above the pliers) into a right angle.

2 Using roundnose pliers, position the jaws in the bend.

3 Bring the wire over the top jaw of the roundnose pliers.

4 Reposition the pliers' lower jaw snugly into the loop. Curve the wire downward around the bottom of the roundnose pliers. This is the first half of a wrapped loop.

5 Position the chainnose pliers' jaws across the loop.

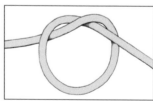

6 Wrap the wire around the wire stem, covering the stem between the loop and the top bead. Trim the excess wire and press the cut end close to the wraps with chainnose pliers.

OPENING AND CLOSING LOOPS OR JUMP RINGS

1 Hold the loop or jump ring with two pairs of chainnose pliers or chain-nose and roundnose pliers, as shown.

2 To open the loop or jump ring, bring one pair of pliers toward you and push the other pair away. String materials on the open loop or jump ring. Reverse the steps to close the open loop or jump ring.

OVERHAND KNOT

Make a loop and pass the working end through it. Pull the ends to tighten the knot.

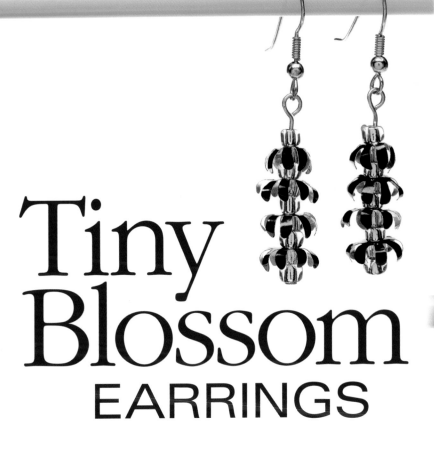

Tiny Blossom
EARRINGS

So quick and easy, you can make several pairs in different colors. These earrings are a good beginner project and a nice introduction to this new craft. Make a pair for all your friends!

1 Prepare cans as in Techniques, p. 7. For each earring, punch out four daisy shapes.

2 Place the shapes on your cork mat and make a hole in the center of each daisy. Move the daisies to a firm surface and hammer them flat.

3 Using roundnose pliers, gently curl each petal toward the uncolored side.

4 On a head pin, pick up two seed beads and a flower. Repeat three times, and then string one more bead.

5 Push the beads and flowers together. Make a plain loop above the beads (Techniques).

6 Open the loop you just made and connect it to an earring wire. Make a second earring to match the first.

DESIGN TIP

For a matching pendant, cut a 1-in. (2.5 cm) length of gold-plated chain and attach a jump ring to one end. Make three flower dangles. Attach a dangle to a top, middle, and bottom link of the chain. Slip a necklace chain through the jump ring.

POSY RING

The easiest way to carry a bunch of flowers, this fun ring jingles nicely when you wear it. All the flowers are made in the same way and attached separately.

You will need:

- aluminum cans
- daisy flower punch, ⅝ in. (15 mm) diameter
- **16–20** 2-in. (5 cm) silver head pins
- **34–38** 6⁰ seed beads
- ring finding with 9 loops
- hammer, cork mat, and self-healing mat
- file
- hole or needle punch
- roundnose pliers
- wire cutters

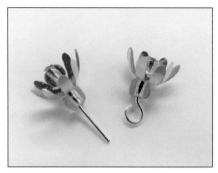

1 Choose any color cans you like, and prepare them as in Techniques, p. 7. Punch out 18 daisies. Place them on a cork mat and make a hole in the center of each shape with a hammer and needle punch. Hammer them flat and file any sharp edges.

2 Pull the daisy petals between your finger and thumbnail to curve them toward the colored side. On a head pin, string a bead, a daisy, and another bead.

3 Push the petals upward into a cup shape around the center bead. Make a plain loop (Techniques).

4 Open the loop and attach the daisy to a loop on the ring. Continue making flowers and adding them to the ring until you have two flowers per loop.

5 Fill in all the spaces you can. The finished ring looks best with lots of flowers.

DESIGN TIP

This variation is red, white, and blue, with beads to match the flowers. I left out the beads behind the flowers to make a smaller, tighter ball.

Chain OF Leaves
EARRINGS

The perfect accompaniment to any floral necklace, these eye-catching dangles are sure to draw attention. Use double-sided leaf shapes and jump rings to make earrings that sway and catch the light as you move.

You will need:

- aluminum can
- leaf punch, ⅝ in. (15 mm) long
- **14** 5 mm jump rings
- pair of earring wires
- hammer, cork mat, and self-healing mat
- file
- hole punch
- superglue
- **2** pairs of chainnose pliers

1 Prepare cans as in Techniques, p. 7. Cut out 14 pairs of leaf shapes, making sure to punch half color-side up and half color-side down. Hammer them flat.

2 Glue two leaves together with super-glue, silver sides together, to make double-sided leaves. After the glue dries, use a hammer and punch to make a hole in each pair of leaves close to the stem.

3 Close three jump rings (Techniques). Open a jump ring, and pick up a leaf and a closed jump ring. Close the ring. (You will be making a chain from jump rings.)

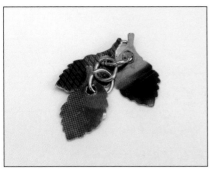

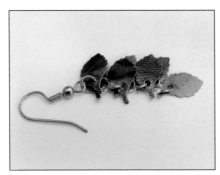

4 Open a jump ring and pick up a leaf, the spare ring on the first leaf, another leaf, and a closed ring. Close the ring. Make sure the leaves are all facing the same way.

5 Repeat Step 4 to add another layer of leaves. For the last layer, pick up a leaf, the ring attached to the chain, a leaf, and an earring wire. Close the ring.

DESIGN TIP

Make longer earrings by adding as many pairs of leaves as you like.

Try a seasonal variation with warm fall colors: Choose a few different shades of orange and red for your leaves and arrange the colors before linking them together.

6 To make the earring hang nicely, slightly curve the leaves with your fingers so they bend around the rings instead of lying dead flat. Make a second earring to match the first.

Snowdrop
EARRINGS

New flowers are delicate reminders of spring, dainty but tough. Wear these earrings during the dark days of winter to remind yourself that sunshine is on the way.

1 Prepare cans as in Techniques, p. 7. Cut out two white flower shapes. Place them on the cork mat, make a hole in the center of each flower shape with the needle punch, and then hammer them flat. Curve each petal slightly towards the silver side between your first finger and thumbnail.

2 On a head pin, string a 8º bead, a flower, a disk bead, and a 4 mm round. Fold three alternate petals over the 8º, then fold in the remaining three petals.

3 Make a plain loop (Techniques). Open the loop to attach an earring wire.

DESIGN TIPS

For bluebells, add a green daisy shape between a blue flower and the 6 mm disk bead. Use roundnose pliers to curl the tips of each petal, then complete as for snowdrops.

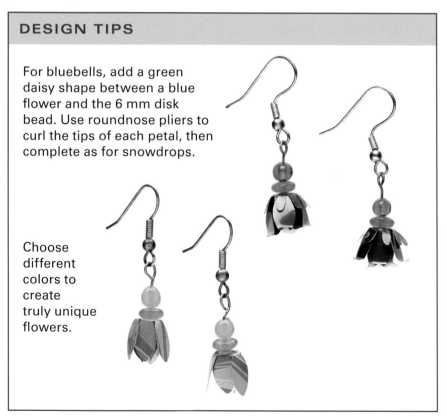

Choose different colors to create truly unique flowers.

Buds AND Leaves
NECKLACE

Mix and match colors according to the season. Attaching flower dangles and leaves to a chain is a quick way to make a necklace. Use a few at the center or cover about half of the chain, as I have here.

1 Prepare cans as in Techniques, p. 7. Cut out 11 flower shapes in a selection of shades. (I chose pinks, creams, and greens for spring.)

2 Place the shapes on a cork mat and make a hole in the center of each flower. Hammer them flat and file the edges of the petals smooth.

3 Pull each petal in turn between your finger and thumb to curve them slightly toward the silver side.

4 On a head pin, string a round bead, a flower, and a flower bead. Fold three alternate petals over the round bead, and then fold in the remaining three petals to form a bud.

5 Make a plain loop (Techniques).

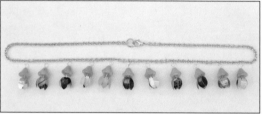

6 **a** Find the center link of the chain and use the loop to attach a bud.

b Arrange the remaining buds next to the chain links, spacing them evenly on either side of the center link. Attach the buds to the chain links.

DESIGN TIP

This version uses richer colors and glass leaves on copper chain for a warm, autumn feel.

7 Punch out 10 pairs of leaf shapes and make 10 double-sided leaves (Techniques). Punch a 1 mm hole in each leaf and attach a jump ring.

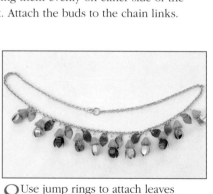

8 Use jump rings to attach leaves between the flower buds.

Fuchsia
EARRINGS

A favorite garden flower also called Lady's Eardrops, fuchsia flowers hang beautifully on the bush. You almost feel that you could pick them off, add an earring wire, and wear them right away.

You will need:

- aluminum cans
- six-petal flower punch, 1 in. (2.5 cm) diameter
- five-petal flower punch 1 in. (2.5 cm) diameter
- **2** 6º silver-lined gold seed beads
- **2** 4 mm round green beads
- **4** 6 mm green disk beads
- **2** head pins
- **2** eye pins
- pair of earring wires
- hammer, cork mat, and self-healing mat
- file
- hole or needle punch
- roundnose and chainnose pliers
- wire cutters

1 Prepare cans as in Techniques, p. 7. Cut out two white six-petal flower shapes and two red 5-petal flowers. Place them on your cork mat and make a hole in the center of each, then hammer them flat.

2 Curve each petal of the white flowers slightly towards the silver side using your thumbnail. Curve the petals of the red flowers lengthways over the barrel of a pen.

3 String a 6º bead on a head pin, trim to 1 in. (2.5 cm), and make a plain loop (Techniques). Attach to an eye pin.

4 On the eye pin, string a red flower, a 6 mm disk, a white flower, a 6 mm disk and a 4 mm round.

5 Make a plain loop. Open the loop to attach an earring wire. Make a second earring to match the first.

DESIGN TIP

Make fuchsias in lots of lovely color combinations.

Bead AND Blossom NECKLACE

You will need:

- aluminum can
- five-petal flower paper punch, 1 in. (2.5 cm) diameter
- **31** 6 mm glass beads
- **22** 10–12 mm glass beads
- 24-gauge (0.5 mm) green craft wire
- Fireline beading thread
- hook-and-eye clasp
- superglue
- hammer, cork mat, and self-healing mat
- file
- hole or needle punch
- roundnose pliers
- wire cutters
- folded towel

Embellish a simply strung necklace with flowers. The flowers can be plain, open blossoms or multi-layered for a more sophisticated look. Use a mixture of beads in your favorite colors.

1 Prepare cans as in Techniques, p. 7. Cut out 11 five-petal flowers and file the edges smooth. Place them on a cork mat and make a hole in the center of each with a needle tool. Use your fingers to curve the petals toward the silver side.

2 **a** Push the ends of the petals up to make a cup shape.

b Cut a 5-in. (13 cm) length of craft wire. Center a 6 mm bead on the wire, and twist the wire ends together to make a wired stem. String a flower, and make a wrapped loop (Techniques). Repeat with all flowers.

3 Arrange the beads and flowers for the center part of the necklace until you are happy with the colors. Work on a folded towel to stop the beads rolling around. Place two 10–12 mm beads between the flowers.

4 Tie Fireline to one half of the clasp with an overhand knot (Techniques). Pick up 10 6 mm beads and a 10 mm bead. Make a knot between the beads a couple of times, glue, and trim the short end.

5 String the beads and flowers following your pattern, then string a 10 mm bead and 10 6 mm beads.

6 Tie the thread to the other half of the clasp. Knot the thread between the beads as before and trim.

DESIGN TIP

For more complicated flowers, use three layers of petals. Curve the petals of the first layer vertically over a pen, then cup them tightly around the center bead.

Shape the middle layer, as in step 2, and curve the last layer slightly. String on behind the first layer and make a wrapped loop on the back.

Summer
Garden
BRACELET

Create your own charm shapes to add to a simple chain bracelet. Make the printing on cans work for you when choosing where to punch out the shapes for this bracelet.

You will need:

- aluminum cans
- six-petal flower punch, ⅝ in. (15 mm) diameter
- four-leaf clover punch, ⅝ in. (15 mm) diameter
- butterfly punch, ½ in. (12 mm) long
- ladybug punch, ⅝ in. (15 mm) long
- 6½ in. (17 cm) chain
- **25** 5 mm jump rings
- lobster claw clasp
- hammer, cork mat, and self-healing mat
- file
- hole or needle punch
- roundnose pliers
- wire cutters

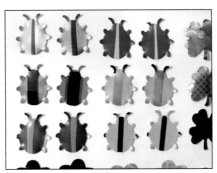

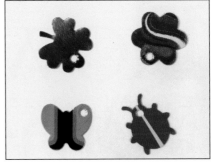

1 Prepare cans as in Techniques, p. 7. Cut out six pairs of each of the four shapes (the charms will be double-sided). Use the pattern on the cans to create fantasy bugs and butterflies.

2 If the shapes are not symmetrical, remember to cut half color-side up and half color-side down.

3 Glue the pairs of shapes together with superglue, then punch a 1 mm hole in each with a hammer and punch. Make the hole about 1 mm from the edge of the shape.

4 Using a jump ring, attach the clasp to one end of the chain. Arrange the charms along the chain, alternating shapes and colors until you like the effect.

5 Use jump rings to attach the charms to the chain, following the pattern you laid out. Make sure to close the rings fully so the charms do not slip out.

DESIGN TIP

For matching earrings, cut two 1-in. (2.5 cm) lengths of chain and attach to earring wires. (Use fine chain for light and wearable earrings.)

Make five double-sided charms for each earring as you did for the bracelet, and attach them to the chain with jump rings. Place one charm at the end of the chain, two halfway up, and two at the top.

Flower Dangle
EARRINGS

Combine flower shapes with glass bead dangles. Start with a simple shape, and vary the colors and shapes of the beads to make a pair of earrings to match every outfit.

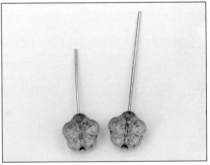

There are many shapes of vertically drilled beads to choose from. For beads that have a hole from front to back (instead of vertically), head pins will not work. Instead, make a chain from jump rings to attach them to the holes in the flower.

1 Prepare cans as in Techniques, p. 7. Cut out four flower shapes and hammer them flat. Glue pairs together with superglue to make two double-sided shapes.

2 With a hammer and 1 mm punch, make four holes in each shape as shown, placing the holes about 1 mm from the edge of the shape.

3 String a bead on each head pin. Cut two head pins shorter by ⅜ in. (1 cm) to make the dangles hang at the correct length.

4 Make a plain loop on the end of each head pin (Techniques). Attach the longest dangle to the center hole, and attach each remaining dangle on either side.

5 Attach an ear wire to the top hole to complete the earring. Make a second earring to match the first.

Flower Link
BRACELET

Colorful flower shapes make an easy-to-wear bracelet. Once you have mastered the technique of joining metal links with jump rings, you can experiment with shapes and patterns.

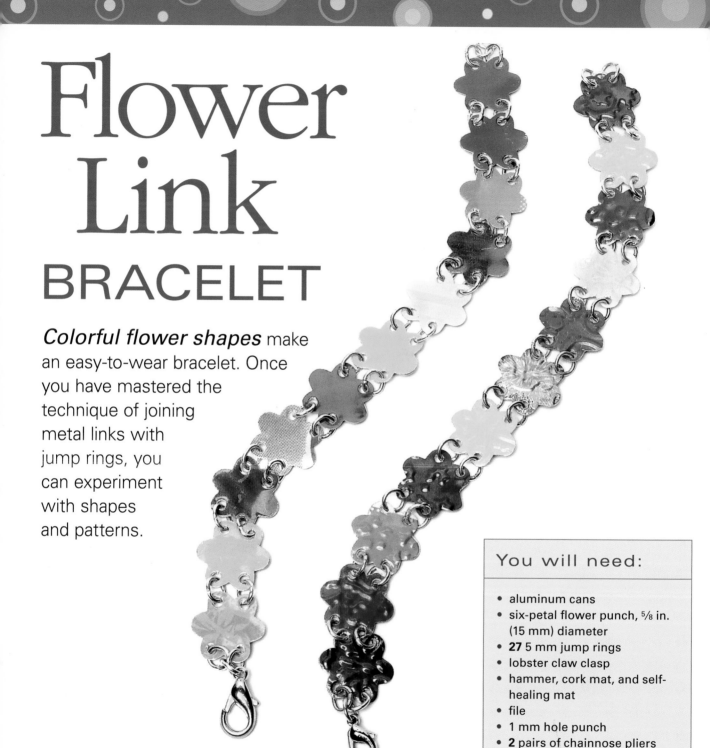

You will need:

- aluminum cans
- six-petal flower punch, ⅝ in. (15 mm) diameter
- **27** 5 mm jump rings
- lobster claw clasp
- hammer, cork mat, and self-healing mat
- file
- 1 mm hole punch
- **2** pairs of chainnose pliers

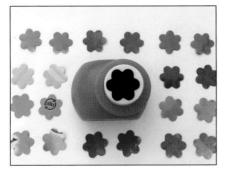

1 Prepare cans as in Techniques, p. 7. Punch out 11 pairs of flower shapes and hammer them flat. Glue pairs of shapes together to make double-sided shapes then texture lightly, if desired.

2 With a hammer and 1 mm punch, make four holes in each shape as shown, placing the holes about 1 mm from the edge of the shape.

3 Attach two shapes together using two jump rings. Close the rings neatly (Techniques). (You may want to squash them into a slight oval with chainnose pliers to keep the thin metal from slipping through the rings.) Repeat for the length of the bracelet.

4 On one end of the bracelet, link a jump ring through each of the two holes. Link a third ring through both rings, pick up a closed ring, and close the open ring.

5 Repeat at the other end of the bracelet, picking up the clasp instead of a closed ring.

DESIGN TIP

Punch shapes from the printed part of the can for a funky look.

Other shapes also work well, like these butterflies.

Daffodil
HAIRPINS

You will need:

- six-petal flower punch,
  1 in (2.5 cm) diameter
- five-petal flower punch,
  1 in. (2.5 cm) diameter
- 2 ⅛ in. (4 mm) rivets or eyelets
- 2 hairpins with flat pads
- two-part epoxy glue
- hammer, cork mat, and self-
  healing mat
- eyelet tool
- file
- hole punch
- eyelet tool

Sunny daffodils always look cheerful. The riveted version has a flat back for gluing on a hairpin or just about any flat surface. Make a whole garden for your tresses!

1 Prepare cans as in Techniques, p. 7. Punch out one of each of the flower shapes. Place them on a self-healing mat and with a hole punch, make a hole large enough to take the rivet in the center of each shape. Hammer flat.

2 Place the rivet on a firm surface, place the five-petal flower color-side up over the rivet, and then add the six-petal flower, color-side down.

3 Using the eyelet tool and hammer, set the rivet. Hammer lightly to flatten the shape.

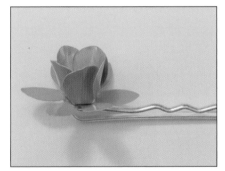

4 Turn the flower over and curve the inner petals lengthwise over the end of a pen. Then ease them together to form the trumpet part of the flower.

5 Using two-part epoxy glue, attach the flower to the flat pad of a hairpin, and leave to dry.

DESIGN TIP

For a wired version, make a wired bead center using a 6º seed bead on a 4-in. (10 cm) length of 24-gauge (0.5 mm) green craft wire. String flowers and a 4 mm round. Use two-part epoxy to glue the round bead to the back of the flower, and let dry. Bend the wire at right angles to the flower. Glue the stems inside a long bead and glue on a brooch back.

Field Poppy
EARRINGS

This is the classic European cornfield flower, signifying re-birth. Single poppies make delicate earrings, but for party time, try a knockout ball of flowers.

You will need:

- aluminum can
- five-petal flower paper punch, 1 in. (2.5 cm) diameter
- daisy flower punch ⅝ in. (15 mm) diameter
- 2 ⅛ in. (4 mm) rivets or eyelets
- 16 6° black seed beads
- 38 in. (.97 m) 24-gauge (.5 mm) green craft wire
- pair of earring studs
- pair of earrings wires
- two-part epoxy glue
- hammer, cork mat, and self-healing mat
- eyelet tool
- file
- hole punch
- chainnose and roundnose pliers
- wire cutters

EARRING STUDS

1 Prepare cans as in Techniques, p. 7. Punch out two five-petal flowers and four daisies. Place them on a self-healing mat, and make a hole large enough to take the rivet in the center of each flower.

2 On a firm surface, place the rivet, one daisy color-side up, the other daisy color-side down, and the five-petal flower color-side down.

3 Using the eyelet tool and hammer, secure the rivet, and then hammer lightly to flatten it.

4 Using roundnose pliers, curl the first row of petals tightly toward the middle. Curve the second row slightly, and then cup the outer petals with your fingers to shape the flower.

5 Using two-part epoxy glue, attach the flower to an earring stud and leave to dry. Make a second earring to match.

EARRING DANGLES

1 Make a wired bead center (Techniques) with a 4-in. (10 cm) length of 24-gauge (.5 mm) craft wire and a black 6º seed bead. String two black daisies and a red five-petal flower, and then make a wrapped loop. Repeat to make eight flowers for each earring.

2 Cut an 6-in. (15 cm) length of wire. String eight wired poppies and center on the wire. Twist the ends together tightly. Trim to about 2½ in. (6.4 cm), make a wrapped loop at the top of the wire, and attach an ear wire. Make a second earring to match.

Tiny
Blossom
BROOCH

You will need:

- aluminum cans
- daisy punch, 5/8 in. (15 mm) diameter
- six-petal flower punch, 5/8 in. (15 mm) diameter
- leaf punch, 5/8 in. (15 mm) diameter
- **6** 6º green seed beads
- sieve brooch finding
- needle and beading thread
- hammer, cork mat, and self-healing mat
- file
- needle punch
- roundnose pliers
- wire cutters

Revisit the tiny blossoms from previous projects, and stitch flowers and leaves to a sieve brooch finding.

1 Prepare cans as in Techniques, p. 7. Punch out nine green leaves and six green flower shapes. and 12 daisy shapes. Move them to a cork mat.

2 With a hammer and needle punch, make holes in each shape as shown: in the center of the flowers and daisies and towards the stem of the leaves. Hammer shapes flat.

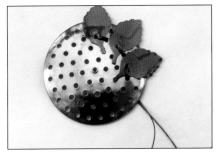

3 Take apart the brooch finding. Thread the needle with 1 yd. (.9 m) of thread, double it, and knot the ends (Techniques). Sew up through a hole in the second ring of holes, up through a leaf, and then down through the next hole.

4 Repeat around the circle, spacing the last few leaves to fit evenly. Stitch around again in the opposite direction to secure the leaves.

5 Stitch up through a leaf and pick up a green flower, two daisies, and a bead as shown. Sew back through the daisy and flower shapes and down through the hole.

6 Repeat around the circle to place five flowers. Use roundnose pliers to curl the petals towards the center of the flowers. (Also curl the two daisies not yet attached.)

7 Sew up through the center hole, pick up the last three shapes and bead, and stitch them down to match the others.

8 Fasten off the thread. Attach the brooch back by bending the small tabs with pliers.

DESIGN TIP

For this ring, omit the leaves around the edge and use four different colors for the flowers.

Sunflower
SET

Brighten up your day with this sunny ring and necklace. They are so quick and easy to make, you could make an entire garden of blooms in no time.

RING

1 Prepare cans as in Techniques, p. 7. Cut out two six-petal flowers and two daisies. Hammer flat.

2 With a hammer and punch, make a hole in the center of each shape large enough to fit the rivet.

3 Place the shapes color-side down over the rivet, first the daisies, then the larger flowers.

4 With a hammer and eyelet tool, set the rivet. Curl the petals slightly, and attach the finished flower to the ring finding with two-part epoxy glue.

PENDANT

1 To make a pendant, layer the shapes onto the rivet as in "Ring," then place a pendant pad with a hole in the center over the rivet.

2 Add a small six-petal flower and set the rivet. String a 7 mm jump ring through the loop on the pad and close it. String the pendant on a necklace chain.

DESIGN TIP

Make a selection of flowers in different colors.

Flowers can be as big or as small as you like.

Link different sizes together to make a show-stopping bracelet.

Gerbera
PENDANT

Create a bold flower with a stitched bead center. Although you can buy ready-made sieve findings, I made my own so I could get exactly the right size and color. As you gain more metalworking experience, you can adapt this method to other projects.

1 Prepare cans as in Techniques, p. 7. Punch out eight drop-shaped petals and two circles in a complementary color. Also cut a ¼ x 1½ in. (6 x 38 mm) strip with scissors. File the petal edges smooth.

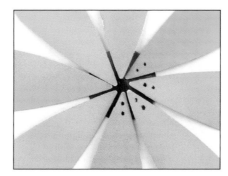

2 Arrange the petals over a circle so they just touch, and mark two spots on each petal with a felt-tip pen just inside the circle. On a cork mat, punch holes on the spots with a needle punch and hammer, and hammer the shapes flat.

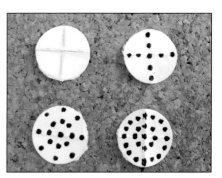

3 With the circle punch, cut a circle from a sticky-back label. Fold it in half twice to find the center, and then mark spots as shown with a fine felt-tip pen.

4 Stick the marked circle to a metal circle, place it on your cork mat, and punch holes with a needle punch. Remove the label and hammer on the back with the rounded hammer end to make a slightly domed shaped.

5 Thread the needle with 1 yd (.9 m) of beading thread, double it, and knot the ends together with an overhand knot (Techniques). Sew up through the center hole, pick up a bead, and go back through the same hole.

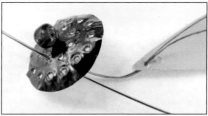

6 Stitch up through a petal through the hole nearest to the point, and up through a hole in the inner circle of holes. Pick up a bead, and go back through the same holes. Repeat for the seven remaining petals.

7 Stitch up through the first petal added, sew through eight beads in a circle to line them up neatly, and then stitch down to the back of the flower.

8 Stitch up through an outer hole petal and hole in the outer ring of holes. Pick up a bead and stitch down through the next hole in the ring, between the petals.

9 Repeat for each petal, adding eight beads, then stitch back in the opposite direction filling in the gaps (16 beads in total).

10 Stitch to the back and fasten off the thread. Fold the petals toward the front of the flowers as shown.

11 Fill the center with two-part epoxy glue and cover with the second circle. Allow the glue to set.

12 Fold the metal strip around a file handle to make an R shape. Glue the ends together and hold with a clothespin until set.

13 Curve the petals toward the back between your first finger and thumbnail. Glue the hanging loop to the back of any petal. String a chain through the loop to finish.

DESIGN TIP

Get a different effect by varying the number of petals. Use the same number of holes in the center circle, but arrange the petals differently when you sew through them.

Fantasy Flower NECKLACE

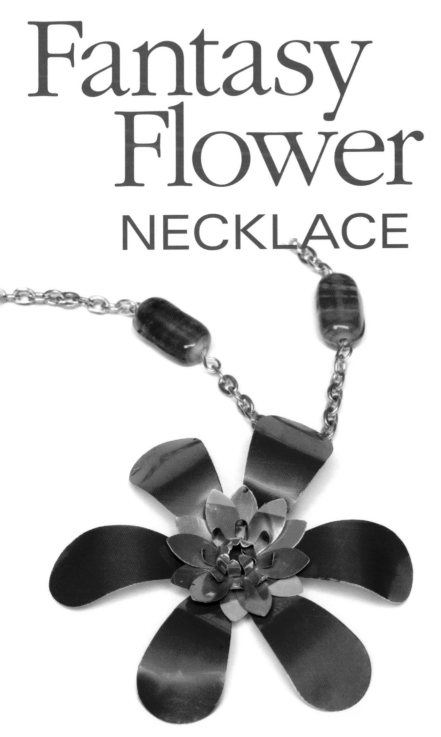

This is the Sunflower Ring's big sister! Make the flamboyant flower as colorful as you like, and try your hand at simple linking to make a necklace from beads and chain to complement the pendant.

1 Prepare can as in Techniques, p. 7. Punch out six drop shapes, two six-petal flowers, two daisies, and two small six-petal flowers. Cut a ¼ x 1½ in. (.5 x 3.2 cm) strip with scissors. File the edges of the drops.

2 Place a thin layer of two-part epoxy glue on the silver side of a small flower, and arrange the six drop shapes so that they are evenly spaced and just touch in the center.

3 Add a little more glue to the tips of the drops and place the other small flower on top (see photo, step 4). Press together firmly and leave to dry. Do not use too much glue, or it will be messy.

4 With a hammer and punch, make holes in all the flower shapes large enough to fit a rivet. Layer the shapes largest to smallest on the rivet, and set with a hammer and eyelet tool.

5 Use roundnose pliers to curl the first layer of daisy petals over the rivet, then curl the second layer slightly. Ease the other petals forward to shape the flower center.

6 Curve the large petals by pulling them between your first finger and thumbnail. Form the metal strip into a hanging loop, as in "Gerbera Pendant," p. 38. Glue the loop to the back of any petal.

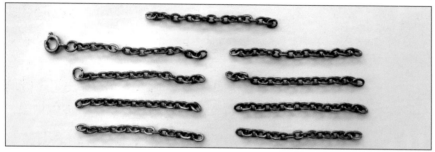

7 Cut the chain into eight 2-in. (5 cm) lengths and one longer piece. Attach the clasp to one of the 2-in. pieces with a jump ring and attach the other jump ring to another 2-in. piece.

8 String a bead on an eye pin and make a plain loop (Techniques). Repeat with the other beads.

9 Attach a bead link to one end of the longer piece of chain. String the chain through the loop on the flower and attach another bead link to the other end of the chain.

10 Attach a piece of chain to each of the bead links, then attach a bead link to each chain.

11 Continue adding beads and chain, ending with the clasp and jump ring.

DESIGN TIP

Different combinations of colors change the look. You need only a few beads to make one of these necklaces.

Daisy
Chain
BRACELET

Release your inner child
with a timeless, carefree design.
This bracelet will last much
longer than the ones made
from real daisy petals.

DESIGN TIP

For matching earrings,
leave out the 10 mm jump
ring and replace the third
daisy with a six-petal
flower shape. Glue a flat-
top earring stud to the back
of the flower with two-part
epoxy glue. Leave to dry.

You will need:

- aluminum cans
- daisy punch, ⅝ in. (15 mm) diameter
- leaf punch, ⅝ in. (15 mm) long (optional)
- **7** rivets or eyelets
- **38** 5 mm jump rings
- **7** 10 mm jump rings
- lobster claw clasp
- superglue
- hammer, cork mat, and self-healing mat
- eyelet tool
- file
- hole punch
- roundnose pliers
- wire cutters

1 Prepare cans as in Techniques, p. 7. Punch out 21 daisy shapes and hammer them flat. With a hammer and punch, make a hole in each shape large enough to fit a rivet.

2 Place a shape over the rivet, color-side down. Squeeze a few drops of superglue around the center, and then place another shape on top, color-side down. Press together to make a complete daisy.

3 Position a 10 mm jump ring on the completed daisy and place a third shape on top.

4 Press the center of the shape firmly against the rivet, inside the jump ring, using roundnose pliers. Set the rivet with a hammer and eyelet tool.

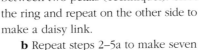

5 **a** Open a 5 mm jump ring and ease it through the 10 mm ring in a space between two petals (Techniques). Close the ring and repeat on the other side to make a daisy link.

b Repeat steps 2–5a to make seven daisy links.

6 Open a 5 mm jump ring and pick up a closed ring and a ring attached to a daisy link. Close the ring. This makes a three-ring chain.

7 Open a 5 mm jump ring and string the end of the three-ring chain and the clasp. Close the ring.

8 Repeat step 6 on the other side of the daisy link; then attach another daisy link in the same way that you attached the clasp. Keep adding daisy links and ring chains until the bracelet will fit around your wrist. (I made 7 daisies in total.)

9 End with a three-ring chain. If desired, add double-sided leaves in between the daisies with jump rings

You can wear the daisy chain plain, or add metal or glass leaves to the chain in between the daisies with jump rings.

Create Colorful Aluminum Jewelry **45**

Apple Blossom
BROOCH

A spray of blossoms with a Japanese feel, this brooch is quite large yet delicate. It takes a while to make, but the individual steps are straightforward.

You will need:

- aluminum can
- five-petal flower punch, 1 in. (2.5 cm) diameter
- leaf punch, ⅝ in. (15 mm) long
- 24-gauge (.5 mm) green craft wire
- 28-gauge (.315 mm) green craft wire
- 5 6º pink seed beads
- 5 6º green seed beads
- brooch back finding
- two-part epoxy glue
- hammer, cork mat, and self-healing mat
- file
- hole or needle punch
- roundnose pliers
- wire cutters

DESIGN TIP

Make a simpler version with only three flowers. Use different colors to match your garden.

1 Prepare cans as in Techniques, p. 7. Punch out five flower shapes and seven pairs of leaf shapes. Make a hole in the center of the flowers with a hammer and needle punch. Curve the petals slightly between your finger and thumbnail.

2 Make wired bead stems with pink beads and 24-gauge (.5 mm) wire 10 in. (25 cm) long. On each stem, string a flower shape and a green bead. Glue the bead to the back of the flower with epoxy glue and leave to dry.

3 Make wired leaves with 28-gauge (.315 mm) wire 5 in. (13 cm) long (Techniques). Take two leaves and twist the wire together. String a flower just below the leaves and secure it by twisting the wires together (see photo in step 4). Make three sets like this.

4 Take two sets of flowers and leaves and twist them together as shown in the photo.

5 Add two single flowers by twisting their stems onto the branch you are forming.

6 Join on the last flower and leaf set, and then add a single leaf close to the join.

7 Trim the wires. At this stage, the last flower and leaf may be loose, but this will be fixed in the last step.

8 Using two-part epoxy glue, attach a brooch back to the center of the branch and leave to dry.

9 Cut a 8-in. (20 cm) length of 28-gauge (.315 mm) wire, start at the branch end, and wrap it around the branch and brooch back to secure. Finish and trim. Twist and adjust the stems and flowers as needed.

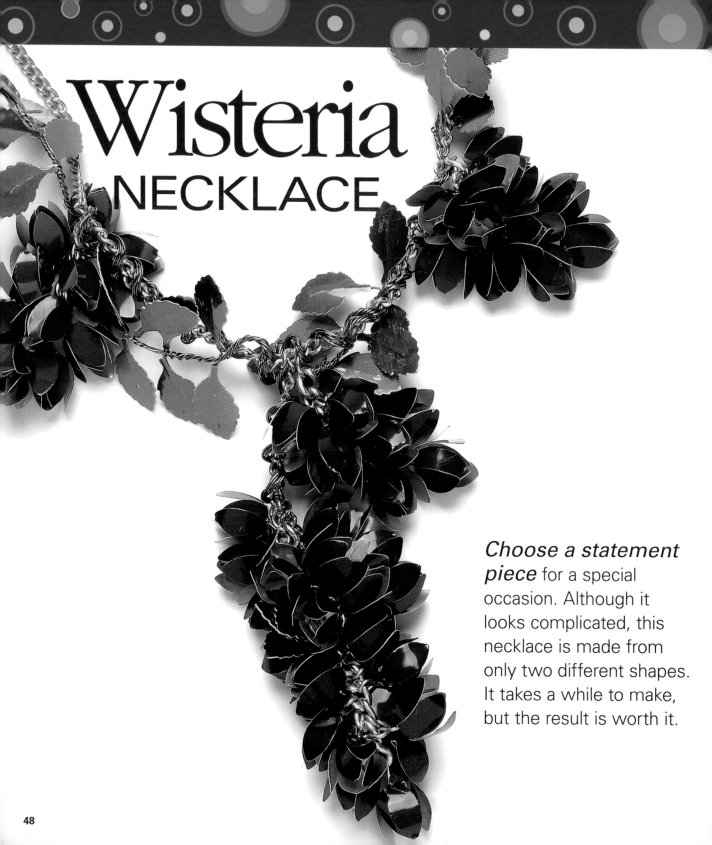

Wisteria
NECKLACE

Choose a statement piece for a special occasion. Although it looks complicated, this necklace is made from only two different shapes. It takes a while to make, but the result is worth it.

FLOWER BUNCHES

1 Prepare cans as in Techniques, p. 7. For each flower bunch, punch out 11 flowers. Make a hole in the center of each flower with the needle tool, then hammer flat. Curve each petal between your finger and thumbnail.

2 On a head pin, string a bead and a flower. Fold three alternate petals over the bead, and then fold in the other three petals to form a bud.

3 Make a plain loop above the flower (Techniques). Repeat for the other flowers.

4 Cut a piece of chain that measures about 1 in. (2.5 cm) (seven links). Attach three flowers to the bottom link, then two to each of the next five links, leaving the top link free. (It is much easier to hold the chain if you thread a bit of scrap wire through the top link.)

5 Make five bunches of flowers.

You will need:

- aluminum cans
- six-petal flower punch, 1 in. (2.5 cm) diameter
- leaf punch 5/8 in. (15 mm) diameter
- **55** 6º seed beads
- **55** 2 in. (5 cm) head pins
- 28-gauge (.315 mm) green craft wire
- 25 in. (64 cm) gold-plated chain with 7 links per inch
- lobster-claw clasp
- **7** 5 mm jump rings
- cork mat, hammer, and self-healing mat
- file
- needle tool
- wire cutters
- chainnose and roundnose pliers
- chopstick or file

LEAF CLUSTER

1 For each leaf, cut out seven pairs of leaf shapes. Make them into seven wired leaves, as in Techniques, making the wire stems about 5 in. (12 cm) long.

2 Take three leaves and twist the wires together as shown. Continue twisting for about ½ in. (1.3 cm).

3 Add a leaf to each side and twist all the wires for another ½ in. (1.3 cm).

4 Add the last two leaves and continue twisting to the end of the wires. Make five clusters in total.

DESIGN TIP

WISTERIA EARRINGS

1 Follow "Flower bunches," steps 1–4. Attach the bunch to an earring wire with a jump ring.

2 Follow steps 6 and 7, using only three leaf shapes to make a small leaflet. Push the stem of the leaflet through the top link of the chain. Wind the wire around the chain three times, then trim the wire and flatten the end with chainnose pliers.

3 Repeat to make a second earring.

ASSEMBLY

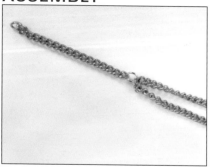

1 Cut a piece of chain about 2 in. (5 cm) long. Attach the clasp to one end of the long chain and a jump ring to the other end. Attach the 2-in. piece to the center of the necklace with a jump ring.

2 Attach flower bunches to the bottom and middle links of the short chain using jump rings. Attach another bunch next to the short chain on the necklace.

3 Attach the remaining two bunches to the necklace about 2 in. (5 cm) on either side of the center.

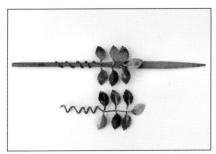

4 Take a cluster and hold it along something narrow, like a chopstick or file. Wrap the wire stem around the handle to form a spiral then gently slide it off. Repeat with the remaining clusters.

5 Carefully twist the spiral stem around the chain so that the leaf sits just beside the flower in the middle of the short chain.

6 Loop the ends of the wire through the jump ring and squeeze them to secure the stem. Make sure there are no sharp ends.

7 Attach clusters to each side of the center. Slide the wires carefully through the center jump ring and spiral them along the chain. Do not secure the ends yet.

8 Now attach a cluster so it sits beside one of the side flowers. Loop the wire ends through the wires from the center leaf and twist them together. Repeat on the other side.

9 Squeeze all the wire ends with chainnose pliers to make sure there are no sharp ends. Take some time to adjust the flowers and clusters so they hang nicely.

Rose
BRACELET

Let roses grow on you!
After a little practice, you will
be able to make classic rose
jewelry for all occasions.

You will need:

- aluminum can
- five-petal flower punch, 1 in. (2.5 cm) diameter
- **7** 4 mm rivets or eyelets
- bracelet finding
- two-part epoxy glue
- hammer, cork mat, and self-healing mat
- eyelet tool
- file
- hole or needle punch
- roundnose pliers
- wire cutters

1 Prepare cans as in Techniques, p. 7. Cut out three flowers and hammer them flat. File any sharp edges. Make a hole in each large enough to take a rivet.

2 Layer the shapes onto the rivet, the first layer color-side up and the other two color-side down. Secure the rivet.

3 Fold up one petal on the first layer and use roundnose pliers to curl the sides in to form a tube.

4 Skip a petal, then curl in the edges of the next petal to fit around the first one.

5 Repeat with remaining three alternate petals on this layer. Now roll the center between your finger and thumb to make a tight bud.

6 On the next layer, hold a petal with your roundnose pliers and fold the edges upwards to cup it lengthwise.

7 Use the pliers to turn back the top edges either side of the middle.

DESIGN TIP

You can attach roses to earrings, rings, pendants, hair clips, and many other findings. To make earrings, fit a rose to a pendant pad with a hole, place it over the rivet on top of the three petal layers, and then add a small flower before securing the rivet. Attach the pad to an ear wire, and repeat to make a second earring.

8 Now gently squeeze the lower part of the petal to make it curve around the center.

9 Working on alternate petals, repeat shaping for all petals on this layer.

10 For the outer layer, use the pliers to curl back the top edge of each petal. You will need seven roses in total.

11 Use two-part epoxy glue to attach the flowers to a bracelet finding and allow to dry.

About the Author

Helen Harle has been interested in crafts for as long as she can remember. She learned to knit and sew at age six and enjoyed knitting toys and making clothes for her dolls. Like many families, there was not much money to spare, so she would unpick unwanted garments and reuse the yarn and fabric for her projects. This continued into her teens, by which time she was making clothes, decorated with beads and embroidery, and restringing broken necklaces into new creations. Helen gets great satisfaction in making something nice from things other people throw away.

Helen lives in Torquay, Devon, England, with her husband, Adrian. They have two grown children, Tanya and Tom, and a new grandson, Christopher. When not making jewelry, Helen loves spending time in her garden, and she is a regular contributor to beading publications.

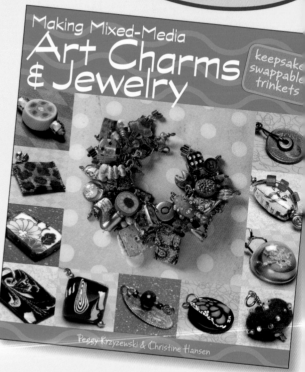